I0210957

Traveling

poems by

Ellen Rosenbloom

Finishing Line Press
Georgetown, Kentucky

.

Traveling

ACKNOWLEDGMENTS

Thank you to Frank Galuszka, Cornelius Eady, Caitlin Jans, Ella Peary, my mom, my sister and of course, Adam, the love of my life.

Publisher: Leah Huete de Maines
Editor: Christen Kincaid
Cover Art: Ellen Rosenbloom
Author Photo: Adam F. Rosenbloom
Cover Design: Elizabeth Maines McCleavy

Order online: www.finishinglinepress.com
also available on amazon.com

Author inquiries and mail orders:
Finishing Line Press
PO Box 1626
Georgetown, Kentucky 40324
USA

Contents

I dedicate this book to my dear father, may his traveling now be filled with serenity and peace—love you always.

"Who so loves believes the impossible."
—Elizabeth Barrett Browning

The Beginnings

Little star opened its mouth
coughed and then let out a big sigh.
Out of its mouth came colors and
textures, ribbons of sound & taste
the beginnings of a world dotted
with glimpses of sky and earth
trees, lakes, oceans & valleys,
fields & mountains & more.

Little star thought about who
should keep up this handiwork—
all of the beauty it had created.
So, out of the ground, it formed
2 bodies with heads and eyes and
mouths. The little star breathed into
their little mouths and they coughed
and let out a sigh and they were alive!

It was so exiting to have these 2 beings.
They started scampering around
the fields and the little star
created other beings for them
to be with—fish and fowl—all
types of animals.

Little star picked up the 2 bodies
by the scruff of their necks
and placed them in a garden
(but we all know how
it goes from there).

For a moment, though, all was
delightful and the world was
brilliant and new.

The Stories

In 1400, it was the plague.
she didn't get lost in sickness
(fortunately) she was with
her cousins & sisters. On the
countryside away from Rome,
telling a tale every night,
keeping the living alive
and entertaining what
was still appalling in the city.

Next, she traveled to 2020
during the Pandemic
without a mask or gloves.
She got lost among the
hospital corridors & the
wall-to-wall patients on
stretchers, in beds, bursting
the sterile-seams of the
white-washed walls.

In 2022, was she sleeping
in the bed? Was she reading
The Decameron by Boccaccio?
Or staring at a painting by
Waterhouse of the plague
of 1400? The ladies and men
sitting outside playing a lute
or a horn and telling stories?

How strange, this 2024...
...How strange that she
and her husband have lived
through a flood, a fire, an
earthquake and the plague.
They have stories to tell.

Light as Feathers

Her feet were light as feathers
and when she ran, she ran with wings to flight.
It was quite a sight to see her—somewhere half
around the moon.

She skipped past the pandemic, the riots,
the capital in flames because when she flew
she sailed past Icarus and barely got singed
by the sun. Her feet, light from day to night
And all through the months and years—
taking flight with grand speckled & silky
wings.

Time went by.
Later, when her feet felt heavy
she would lower her wings and
drop down to earth to take care
of the bills, the groceries, the dishes
and making the bed. This is what
she chose for being wed to someone
she loved & loved & loved.

For the time being, though, she traded
in her silky wings & feathered feet
for simple tights and a dress
and heavy, practical shoes.
But once, harmonizing her happy
marriage and the everyday, she
would take inspiration and fly again—
Soar above the clouds and stars,
barely touching Mars—taking
love and art to be as one. As one.

What is Love but…Charlotte (in Yellow)

In 1800: She and Charlotte Perkins Gilman are too busy
now: with a blade they are scraping out Charlotte's face
to escape the yellow wallpaper and she is getting free. (*Yippee!*)

Her husband is approaching. She and Charlotte jump
out the window now, it's 1892. And they land softly
on the lush green grass below. They are covered
in yellow: yellow wallpaper scraps, yellow shavings,
a ruler, tape, glue—a blade. Charlotte's face
is covered in yellow ash—a mask: she pulls it off.

And she and Charlotte are running free through
the velvety grass. At last it's almost evening.
They've pulled it off. *They've pulled it off.*

Later, in 2024, they get dehydrated and slake their thirst
with wine in tall glasses decorated with mirth and more
flowers and vases. Come now… the baby is sleeping…
do they need to go back—back to the house to the little
one? O is Charlotte, now her—now she—filled with
responsibility? Charlotte *must* go back. Her senses are
coming back to her. She loves her husband. With nerve,
she shakes away the yellow and calmly walks into
the house, her bones burning like an inferno on the inside.
Calmly walking up the path
the life-fire burning inside her head.
Yellow candle. Yellow flames. Yellow fire.
Everything was Yellow.

Being Small

She took a walk through the path between these 2 grand rocks
In Arizona. It reminded her of being in Peru at Saskywamen
and how tall the boulders were there. Carefully, she stationed
herself in front of a formation which looked like it had a door
which her guide joked, could lead to another dimension.
Her husband was sick back at the hotel. The only request
he had was for handkerchiefs. After the baffling boulders
(like how did they get there and who In the world could have
moved them?) She looked miniature beneath them when
she saw the picture the guide took.

Later, back in town in Cusco, the guide led her to a small shop
and in hand motions and a little Spanish, the shopkeeper
produced 2 glowing white handkerchiefs—she bought them
her mind still buzzing with the: *how did it all happen and how
were the boulders moved?*

The guide joked: Aliens moved them through telekinesis. It seemed
as plausible an explanation as any…

And now, dwarfed by the giant striated orange and white rock—
like the pattern of a melted creamsicle on concrete—she felt that
same sense of little-ness walking along this path between the 2
great rocks. Mystery without revelation—it was so frustrating but
also awe-inspiring and was the type of unknown which sinks into
your brain and has your wheels turning.

When the guide and the driver dropped her back at the hotel, she
stopped in front of a monk who was weaving in the lobby and bought
a handkerchief square from him too. Her husband was happy
with the purchases, but couldn't believe the picture of her,
beneath the boulders and how small she was.

In Honor of Little Plantie

I bought the Cyclamen that sits on my windowsill
almost 2 years ago. It was supposed to be a present
for my mom, but the day my husband and cousins
went to see my mom in New Jersey, we were in
the car when I realized I forgot it. I was so distressed.
It was Mother's Day and now I was empty-handed.
My father had died the year before in August and
I wanted Mother's Day to be special for my mom—
especially this year. My husband was quick to
find a flower shop in her neighborhood and so
we ordered an orchid for her—to be delivered
that afternoon.

She loved the orchid but worried that she
wouldn't be able to take care of it properly—
We all assured her that she would. "I don't know,"
she said, "I still wish that I could've taken better care
of dad—at least a bit better—."
"Oh, mom," I said, "You took care of him just fine.
His body gave up and it was his time—"
"Yes, yes," she said and put the orchid at the center
of the dining room table.

I was terrified that I'd kill the Cyclamen, so I
watered faithfully, started talking to her and
named her "Little Plantie." I had never really
had a plant before, except a cactus I had growing
up that I named Agnes. Agnes just fell over one day
and that was the end. But Little Plantie started to bloom.
And she has actually bloomed ever since. I weed
her and pull out the dead leaves and flowers
and she keeps on blooming. I love Little Plantie.
She brings me so much joy when I look at her
On the windowsill in front my desk.

My mother was able to nurture the Orchid.
She put it on her terrace and it was thriving
And blooming too. For a while, that is. Last
I saw her, the Orchid was nowhere in sight.
"Mom," I said, "Is the Orchid alright?"
"Yes," she said, "She's just sleeping for now—
That's what they say to do during the winter
months, but she'll bloom again."
"I know she will," and I squeezed my mom's hand,
"Every being has a season—like the song says."
"Yes," Mom said.

Elk or Springbok?

He had a bunch of statues in his apartment, one of
an Elk with a sprig of twig coming out of its head.
We had a lot to talk about, we had just started living
together and I was included in the family trip to South Africa.

There, we saw a Springbok pinioned to a branch in a tree.
The guide had said to look up and there we saw the dead
Springbok, half his hindquarters gone. Below, a Hyena
was licking his lips waiting for any part of the animal to fall
so he could eat. "Who killed him?" My (now husband's) father
asked. "It was a Cheetah, who's probably down at the lake
slaking his thirst." The guide said.

But there was other news to talk of like where to place
the Elk statue in our new apartment? I had some sculptures
that needed a place too.

"I feel like I witnessed something awful." I said to my husband
after seeing the Springbok. He nodded and took out his phone
to start snapping pictures of the scene.

That night I could hardly sleep, I kept seeing that Springbok.
"Adam," I said, "Do you think that Cheetah will be punished
For killing the Springbok?"
"I don't know. I think the Cheetah just thought: food for dinner."
"Yes," I said, "It's wild out there."

But back to the apartment: the Elk statue reminded me of
the Springbok and I didn't want it in our home.
"That's okay," Adam said, "I'd rather have a bust
of the Maltese Falcon instead."
"Yes," I said, "I can live with that."

Not Lions

It's not that I would assume a fetal position—It was
just that when we saw the lions in South Africa
I wished I could.

I do not like lions. The guide on our trip would try
and track them down. We would ride for hours
looking for the lions. Once the guide got out with
his shotgun and left everyone in the jeep while he
went into the bush to try and track them down.

He came up empty handed that time. But then
there was the next time—when he found the lions
and our jeep and about three others were parked
around the pack. He told us to be silent and just
observe and take pictures. Mostly the lions
slept and stretched. I was terrified someone
would cough or sneeze or even blurt something out
in all the silence, and that would be that—
the lions would pounce on us and it would all
be over. I don't like lions—they scare me.

That time no one coughed or sneezed or blurted out
anything. After about fifteen minutes of watching
and taking pictures of the lions, I suggested to
the guide that we leave. He said, "No worries,
the lions just think of us like Paparazzi and they
really have no interest in us."

There were other dangers while we were there,
The day before we arrived at the camp, they told us
that a man got too close to a giraffe and the
giraffe kicked him a fatal blow. But mostly,
I just didn't like the lions.

Later, when we were back in the states,
my husband showed me a video of a lion
jumping into the back of a jeep in South Africa.
He clung to one of the people and the guide
had to carefully unfurl the lion from the person.

Luckily the guide didn't have to shoot the lion—
as much as I don't like them, I wouldn't want to see
them dead.

"Lucky, you didn't show me this video before our trip."
I said to my husband.
"Yes, I knew you'd have never come if you had seen it."
"That's for certain!"

It's been a joke among our family that I don't like lions.
Nieces and nephews will talk about it and laugh heartily.

When we got back, I just felt lucky to have survived.

In Capri

We drove up to the top of the cliff
and got out to go into a little shop.
It was part grocery store, part café.
We took the stairs up to the 2nd
floor, greeted the chef who gave us
a cooking lesson. We made dough
from water, eggs and flour, rolled out
our concoctions and filled them
with cheese that we sweetened
with honey and also added other
spices. We put the raviolis together.
The chef put them into boiling water
and cooked for 10 minutes. Meanwhile,
we sat in the back of the café overlooking
vines with flowers and hills. They served us
our creations and we bit in and chewed—
delicious.

The cheese was just the right
balance between sweet & savory.
They served us many more courses—
the food they prepared.

So
delicious.
So
wonderful.

From vegetables from their garden
out back to pasta and meats of all kinds.
The food was heavenly. So that's what
we did in Capri, one fine summer
afternoon. They let us keep the aprons
we cooked in with a recipe for Limoncello
(which we both agreed was not our
favorite) but the aprons were pretty
with the lemons and the text.

Otherwise, we found Capri to be
crowded and hard to navigate.
We got lost more than once walking
the streets near our hotel.

What is Left

After dad passed
I was inspecting the objects he left on his desk,
I encountered her: a ceramic face. Last, I had seen
her, she was broken into a hundred pieces—all the parts
saved in a plastic bag. Like how my heart felt that day
he passed—broken into a hundred pieces, but she was
all of apiece. He had carefully glued all the fragments
together and she was now whole. Like me: the heart mends,
but it takes time—I think of him and how we were all together
that marked day of his death. The day he left.

She's now on my desk and I look at her from time to time—
that's what is left. But so much more—memories and more.

I Wrote a Poem Today

Today I wrote a poem so personal I will not share it (but
I did share it with my husband who liked it but wondered
if others may think it maudlin.) My mother told me she has
macular degeneration but there is a shot she can get
in her eye once a month. I worry about her… and it's so ironic
because she is so visual. She draws and designs and fills up
her whole apartment with her creations. What would she do
if she couldn't see? Maybe it won't come to that…
I worry the shot will be painful—I asked her if they give
a painkiller—she said she didn't know. It's hard to get old.
I watched my dad get old and basically decompose, piece
by piece. His brain was on fire, he was so aware of everything.
Everything. All of it was too much…one part of him giving up
at a time. When he died, I saw a butterfly swoop into the room,
spread its wings and soar from wall to window to door. I thought
it was him—finally free from the prison his body had become—
now beautiful…
now free.

Mom will be okay. She's strong and has many friends
and her small family to rely on.
My family with my husband is pretty big
And she is included with them too.
She will be alright. She still drives and takes care
of herself and is stronger and smarter than people
decades younger. She and I compare *New York Times*
Wordle and Connections scores every day. She will be okay.

The Copywriter as an Old Dog

The Copywriter lies on the velvet couch with her feet up.
She sips from a cup of broth and takes a spoon to her lips
And sips and sips. The days of writing copy are coming
to a close—all those clothes, the housewares, the shoes
all a blur to amuse the past. There is something sad
in the way it all ends—simply too old to scold herself
about the way things might have been. Could there be
one last job to put the finishing touches on her story?
Surely, the sun has not set yet and surely the horizon
is not giving up—who is to say who you touch?

The sun never goes away for more than a day,
Isn't that a fact? The last boss lacked some tact
And was far from the truth—sitting on a leather
chair in his restaurant booth, sipping broth, cozy
in his fuzzy sweater. With all the buzzing about
how she would write stellar copy: take a snobby
moment from the manager who said, (syrup sweet)
"*You have such great ideas*, but we have to change
all of it to conform to the haul of it. The lot of it."

Beauty is as beauty does. On the precipice of
one thing lies another—now dormant, now
bitter sweet. There's one chance left? Or
would that be more? Don't think of it as a chore,
think of it as combing the dog's hair—all matted
what's the matter? Matter flitting about
like purple dust. She'll be okay on this day.
Now another. Now another.
Now another.

Waiting

Waiting, waiting and waiting when
thinking and waiting about something.
Things take time ahead of the curve.
The camber of the road—the contour
of the streets and the many names
it's been named. I wonder why
it all takes time? Be patient. *Be patient.*

Be a patient in the hospital—all white
gowns with purple geometrics and little
yellow socks before the surgery.
*It'll take about an hour—you won't be
aware of the time.* Your husband has to be
patient. Bides his time by visiting
the gift shop, the café, a flower shop.
He paces.

Time to practice patience for the new job
to start—*when will my manager contact me
to onboard already?*

My husband paces the tiled floor
and waits. Like I wait and wait
practicing to be patient (as a patient—
as a citizen of the country, as a lark).
I can call about the job? Better wait
and practice patience—she will get back
to you. She will. And you will recover
from the anesthesia.

Salmon Bisque

When we first met, my (now) husband
said he'd make his "famous" salmon bisque.
He put on his cute apron with the stripes
and said, "You can help."
I said, "Yes, what do I do?"
He showed me all the ingredients:

2 7-Ounce Salmon Steaks
Half and Half
Almond Milk
Sherry
White Onions
Mushrooms
Chicken Broth

Seasoning:
Fresh Garlic
Garlic Powder
Garlic Salt
Pepper
Dill

He put the spices in a tiny, tiny Pyrex bowl and put that aside.
He took the chicken broth and mushrooms
and put them in a blender, "You blend it up!"
I pressed the button and voilà it was pureed.
He chopped up and added onions and I pressed
the button again and voilà it was pureed.
He got out a cutting board and placed the salmon
on it, "But" he said, "Before that we have to pour
the puree into a pan to cook. When it starts to bubble,
add in a ½ a cup of half and half,
and ½ a cup of almond milk and stir with a whisk."
I did and then it started to cook.
Meanwhile, he sliced the salmon into chunks
and he put it into the mixture in the pan.
"You season it," he said.

So, I put in all the spices from the Pyrex bowl,
and while the concoction started to boil, I added in
the fresh garlic that he had put through the garlic press
and added in the dill. "As a penultimate step,"
he pulled out some paprika and put a dash of that in and
then added a touch of cayenne pepper. I stirred.
"As a final touch," he said, "Here," and poured in some Sherry.
We waited for it to cook, about 5 minutes. (So the salmon
wouldn't be too tough.) I set the table with napkins. (which
were actually paper towels folded in half) and silverware and
plates. It smelled really wonderful.
He put a portion in a bowl for each of us.
We sat down to eat. And that was that.
We had a delightful meal.
And that was the start
of a beautiful relationship.

Home is a Bootleg Beast Song

Our home is a bootleg beast song
and we can't seem to erase the
growling and grandeur and singing
morning noon and night. My husband
sings all the time, it's his profession
after all and he does voiceovers so we
all have accents and characters—many
beasts & evil men, monsters and
rodents & again, more polymorphous
beasts.

It's bootleg because we can't seem
to delete the personalities of the many
creatures who reside with us at home
and we have to charge double for the
ever-present beast-song sound stealing.
for friends and family who come to visit.
It's like living in a cave—all the time!
But honestly, we laugh a lot and love it.
We wouldn't want it any other way…
Who's to say it could be any other way?
It's just here in the cave at our home with
the bootleg beast song.

Lash Tremble Drift

Best to think of others
not simply mothering mothers—
or fathers who have passed not too very
long ago.

She
thinks of husbands, brothers and sisters
Simply a wet lash from a good cry,
a certain tremble at the reality of loss…
and the quivering drift between lovers
and siblings.

Know this, it lasts—the (wet) lash
The (certain) tremble and the
(quivering) drift.

Bring it all together—take this morning
for example: the love for a husband
the love for brothers and sisters
the love for a mother—however
she mothers.

The Beast

He was the definite beast from "Beauty and the Beast."
He was ugly and ill-kempt and sucked on his fingers.

Maybe I wasn't the most beautiful "Beauty" but
I kept thinking he would grow to love me, but

he never did. And once when I hugged him, he
patted my back like a little dog.

There were others that I dated—but they were
all wrong: one tried to kiss me goodnight

and he missed my lips and landed on my shoulder.
There were others, like the guy who said: "This

is not a match." (And I couldn't agree more.)
There was the one who told me I was boring,

when in fact he had been the bore.
A few more—all wrong… So, although the beast

was not such a catch, he was reliable and
honest (I thought) and when he sang

along to the radio as we drove through the city
even though his voice was all off-key—It was endearing.

There were many times I'd think about what it would be
like once he started to love me, but it never happened.

We went out every other week—to dinner, to a movie.
He'd bring his father with him sometimes and we'd all

drink coffee and eat donuts and talk in my apartment.
I have to admit, I was always so astonished at how

ugly he was—his face, the straggly hair, his sparse beard,
his ill-fitting clothes. It would just be a week since

I saw him last and it was always so surprising,
shocking really.

Then he called out of the blue and said,
"I've met her, the one."

"Oh?" I said, "Well, now that's enough."
"What, you don't want me to be happy?"

"That's enough," I repeated. "That's all."
Weeks later I met my husband. It was a text

from a website that turned into a 2-hour call.
We agreed to meet. And although I chickened out

on the first date. (I just didn't think I could
go through it all again.) He called again and

I realized he was different. We met a week later
and the sparks were immediate.

Then weeks turned to months and now
years. And now, like a prince, I'm always astonished

by how handsome he is and how charming and
how happy we are together.

Ellen Rosenbloom was born on an air force base in Clovis, New Mexico where her father was a surgeon. Her family lived in the Bronx, Brooklyn and New Jersey. She moved to NYC for college at Parsons School of Design and the New York Studio School and never looked back. She met her best friend, favorite person and husband, Adam ten years ago. They reside on the Upper Eastside in Manhattan. She has a pet Cyclamen plant and a dollhouse she has carefully been renovating and decorating. She has worked as a Copywriter for over 15 years. Ellen received her MFA in Poetry from the New School and has a BS from Skidmore College in Fine Art. She has studied poetry at the 92nd Street Y and at The Writer's Workshop @ Author's Publish. Her poems have been published in many literary journals and websites. She has also written a novel and novella, and short stories. Her first chapbook of poems, "*Past Life Recall*" was published by Bottlecap Press. She is over the moon that her chapbook, *Traveling* is published by Finishing Line Press. Stay tuned for her full length collection, *Passing Through* forthcoming from Finishing Line Press.